Worker safety should always be the number one priority of every company. Toolbox talks should be conducted on a regular basis to educate workers on safe work practices and stay compliant with regulations regarding safety and training.

Safety toolbox talks are important to building a strong safety culture and reinforcing your company's commitment to protecting your workers. Holding toolbox talks can prevent workers from getting complacent and avoid taking safety for granted.

Conduct toolbox talks on a monthly basis to reinforce your company's focus on safety. Toolbox talks, sometimes referred to as tailgate meetings or safety briefings, are short, informal safety meetings held at the start of a day or shift.

Toolbox talks are a great way to reinforce safety basics, focus on high-risk scenarios and to inform workers about changes to the job and/or working conditions that may have occurred. Be sure to discuss any accidents or injuries that have occurred and how they could have been prevented.

These simple tips can help you in your toolbox talk delivery:

Practice makes perfect

Yes, it's a cliché - but it's true. If you want to communicate a subject well, you need to know it well yourself. Reading off a script will not hold the attention of your audience, so get to know the presentation, read through it a few times, familiarise yourself with the format and structure of the talk you want to deliver.

Practice first and your talk will go much smoother - the more you do, the less you will need to practice.

Stay on topic

Try not to get sidetracked by other subjects or topics. Toolbox talks should focus on one subject, if there is another important subject that comes up and it doesn't require immediate attention, use it as the subject for your next toolbox talk. If it does require urgent attention, finish your toolbox talk, and address the issue afterwards.

If you try to cover more than one topic or too much in a talk, then the delivery will be diluted, and the message could get lost in the middle.

Pace yourself

You need to keep your audience's attention with a short, direct toolbox talk - but that doesn't mean you should rush what you are saying. Monitor the speed at which you are talking and keep at a nice steady pace.

It's better to deliver just the important information in a clear way, rather than try to rush through lots of information that gets forgotten.

Keep it simple

Avoid jargon and make sure your talk is easy to follow. Break the subject down into key sections, for example, an introduction, key points and key safety measures.

Use simple words and phrases and try to avoid technical language - or explain if you do need to use it.

Consider new or inexperienced workers, also give consideration to workers where English is not their first language.

Present positively

If you want others to be interested in what you have to say, you need to be interested in what you have to say. Show enthusiasm for the topic, you should aim to deliver a clear message and get your workers to understand the importance of good health and safety practices on site.

People will be more inclined to listen to a positive talk, and the toolbox talk should be all about proactive positive attitudes towards health and safety on site.

Engage and involve

Make sure you give your audience plenty of eye contact throughout the talk, and that you are speaking loud enough to be heard by everyone. If people can't hear you or don't feel engaged, they will switch off before you finish.

Speak then listen

Some of the most important outcomes from your toolbox talk will come from the questions and feedback you receive from your workers. Communication is a two-way process, so make sure you show your workers that you are interested in their questions, thoughts and opinions and that you value their feedback.

Give them plenty of opportunities to speak up and be heard. Try asking for input, such as workers own experiences of the topic, to get the conversation going.

Check everyone understands

Make sure that the workforce has understood the toolbox talk. Don't just ask if they have understood - it is far easier to say yes than no, even if they don't understand fully. Ask questions on the subject area and run through various aspects of the talk again if required.

This goes hand in hand with engaging your team and getting them involved in the talk.

Topic: Hot Work Permits

A Hot Work Permit is required for any temporary operation involving open flames or producing heat and/or sparks. This includes, but is not limited to, welding, burning, cutting, brazing, grinding and soldering. The Hot Work Permit is really nothing more than a formal checklist to ensure that potential safety issues are addressed in the area you will be doing the work and that someone else agrees it is safe to do the work.

Such work can create heat and sparks which could ignite nearby items unless they are protected. Requirements of the hot permit include things like:

- Floors will be swept clean.
- Flammable liquids, dust, lint, and oily deposits will be removed.
- Ducts and conveyor systems will be protected or shut down to prevent sparks from being carried to other combustibles.
- All combustibles will be removed where possible; otherwise, area will be protected with fire resistive tarpaulins or metal shields.
- Portable fire extinguisher, suitable for the type of possible fire, will be readily available at the work area.

Depending on the area and the work being done a firewatch person may be needed in the area during and after the work is completed.

Some think of the Hot Work Permit as just another piece of paper to fill out while trying to get the job done. However, enough fires have occurred during these types of operations that a formal checklist is required. The hot work permit helps us all ensure that the area is safe for such operations so that we have a place to return to work to tomorrow.

Topic:		
Instructor:	Location:	
Printed Name	**Signature**	**Date**

Topic: Hand Injuries: Lacerations

In a recent study of hand injuries the leading cause of injury was contact with cutting or piercing objects, most often pieces of metal, razors and knives, power tools and nails. Fingers and hands were the most-injured body parts among the construction workers in this study, accounting for one-third of emergency room visits. About 15 percent of these injuries were amputations, partial amputations, crushes and fractures. About 63 per cent involved a laceration.

So how can we reduce hand injuries? A recent study found that wearing gloves reduced the relative risk of injury by 60 percent. We have seen here in our own facility and through the corporation that the wearing of cut-resistant gloves and cut-resistant sleeves when handling or working around cut hazards had dramatically reduced lacerations.

The study also showed that workers reported that they had worn gloves only 27 percent of the work time, and only 19 percent reported wearing gloves at the time of the injury. Gloves are only effective when you wear them.

To reduce the chance of injury when working around cut hazards it is important that you wear the cut-resistant gloves and sleeves. They are made of Kevlar or Dyneema and offer cut resistance to sharp objects. Understand, they are certainly not cut-proof, however they afford you much protection when working with and around sharp items such as:

- Utility knives
- Saw blades
- Dies
- Knives
- Sheet Metal
- Glass
- And similar cut hazards

Topic:		
Instructor:	Location:	
Printed Name	**Signature**	**Date**

Topic: Eye Injuries and Prevention Safety Talk

Our eyes are one of our greatest assets. They give us the ability to see the world around us. If we do not protect our eyes from injuries while at work we could easily lose that ability. There are an estimated 2,000 eye injuries every single day on the job according to the CDC. These incidents cost employers over $300 million dollars per year. It is important to eliminate or engineer out the hazards that could pose hazards to our eyes at work. Many hazards to our eyes on a worksite cannot be fully eliminated so proper eye protection is also critical.

Common Hazards that Cause Eye Injuries on the Job

- Flying dust
- Flying debris
- Chemicals
- Blunt trauma to the eye
- Burns due to UV exposure, such as welder's flash

Best Practices to Avoid Injuries to the Eyes

- Identify all of the potential eye hazards in your work area and for your specific work tasks. Ensure there are proper safeguards in place to prevent an eye injury. If there is a safeguard missing, stop the work task and correct the problem.
- Eliminate or lessen the chance of getting something into your eye by avoiding being in the line of fire. One quick example is standing upwind of debris or dust blowing around the work area.
- Always wear approved safety glasses, face shield, or goggles when needed. The type of PPE needed will depend on the work task. Three out of every five victims of eye injuries on the job were not wearing any eye protection.
- If there is welding activities going on, wear proper eye protection and ensure there is a protective barrier in place to protect other employees in the area from UV exposure.
- If you get something in your eye do not rub or scratch it. Rubbing the eye can cause scratching of the cornea resulting in injury. Find an eye wash station or saline bottle to rinse out the object.
- If you get a chemical in your eyes, remove your contacts if there is any in and begin to rinse your eyes out.

Topic:

Instructor: Location:

Printed Name	Signature	Date

Topic: Hand Safety and Injury Prevention Safety Talk

We use our hands for virtually every task we do at work and because of this fact they are commonly injured on the job. Keeping our hands and fingers out of harm's way at work is critical. A serious injury to an individual's hands or fingers results in a huge negative impact on their ability to work and overall quality of life. While gloves are the most common form of PPE found in the workplace, hand injuries are still the second leading type of injury on the job.

Hand Injury Statistics

- There are 110,000 lost time cases due to hand injuries annually.
- 1 million workers are treated in an ER for hand injuries annually.
- 70% of workers who experienced a hand injury were not wearing gloves.
- Another 30% of victims had gloves on, but they were damaged or inadequate for the work task.

Three Common Types of Hand Injuries

1. Lacerations are the most common type of hand injuries. Lacerations are due to sharp objects or tools. Often inadequate gloves are used during an activity that involves a sharp tool. A glove with Kevlar is effective in protecting the hand against a cutting or slicing motion. A straight stab motion can still easily penetrate these gloves. Caution needs to be used when using any tool that can easily penetrate the skin.
2. Crush injuries are usually due to employees placing their hands in the line of fire between two objects or in a rotating piece of equipment. Pinch points on equipment or tools also commonly lead to crush injuries.
3. Fractures occur when there is a sudden blow to the bones in the fingers or hands. Motor vehicle accidents often cause fractures to the hands. Another common cause of fractures is an individual extending out their hands to catch themselves from a fall.

Safe Work Practices

- Use tools to remove your hands from the line of fire when doing a work task that could result in injury to your hands or fingers. Using tools such as push sticks when using a table saw is an example that removes your hands from the line of fire.
- Avoid using fixed open blade knives. There are safety knives that limit the length of the blade exposed. They also have a safety feature that retracts the blade when pressure is let off the handle or switch that controls the blade.
- Never put your hand in an area where you cannot see it.
- Always wear the proper gloves for whatever work task you are doing. Understand the limitations of your gloves and what work tasks they are appropriate for.
- Never work on an energized piece of equipment. Lock and tag out the equipment to ensure there will not be unintentional start up while you are working on the equipment.

Topic:		
Instructor:	Location:	
Printed Name	**Signature**	**Date**

Topic: Hand Safety and Injury Prevention Safety Talk

We use our hands for virtually every task we do at work and because of this fact they are commonly injured on the job. Keeping our hands and fingers out of harm's way at work is critical. A serious injury to an individual's hands or fingers results in a huge negative impact on their ability to work and overall quality of life. While gloves are the most common form of PPE found in the workplace, hand injuries are still the second leading type of injury on the job.

Hand Injury Statistics

- There are 110,000 lost time cases due to hand injuries annually.
- 1 million workers are treated in an ER for hand injuries annually.
- 70% of workers who experienced a hand injury were not wearing gloves.
- Another 30% of victims had gloves on, but they were damaged or inadequate for the work task.

Three Common Types of Hand Injuries

4. Lacerations are the most common type of hand injuries. Lacerations are due to sharp objects or tools. Often inadequate gloves are used during an activity that involves a sharp tool. A glove with Kevlar is effective in protecting the hand against a cutting or slicing motion. A straight stab motion can still easily penetrate these gloves. Caution needs to be used when using any tool that can easily penetrate the skin.
5. Crush injuries are usually due to employees placing their hands in the line of fire between two objects or in a rotating piece of equipment. Pinch points on equipment or tools also commonly lead to crush injuries.
6. Fractures occur when there is a sudden blow to the bones in the fingers or hands. Motor vehicle accidents often cause fractures to the hands. Another common cause of fractures is an individual extending out their hands to catch themselves from a fall.

Safe Work Practices

- Use tools to remove your hands from the line of fire when doing a work task that could result in injury to your hands or fingers. Using tools such as push sticks when using a table saw is an example that removes your hands from the line of fire.
- Avoid using fixed open blade knives. There are safety knives that limit the length of the blade exposed. They also have a safety feature that retracts the blade when pressure is let off the handle or switch that controls the blade.
- Never put your hand in an area where you cannot see it.
- Always wear the proper gloves for whatever work task you are doing. Understand the limitations of your gloves and what work tasks they are appropriate for.
- Never work on an energized piece of equipment. Lock and tag out the equipment to ensure there will not be unintentional start up while you are working on the equipment.

Topic:		
Instructor:	Location:	
Printed Name	**Signature**	**Date**

Topic: Lack of Time Safety Talk

There are many different sources of pressure individuals face at work for getting the job done. Time, or the lack of it, is a major driver in whether or not workers feel that they need to rush to get a job complete. It is important to plan work accordingly to avoid having to rush work tasks.

Sources of Time Pressures on the Job

There are many reasons why there is not enough time to get work done or at least the perception that there is a lack of time. Some reasons to consider:

- Poor preplanning- A lack of planning is a major factor in whether or not employees have to rush to get work done. Poor preplanning leads to a huge number of issues on the job and often results in safety-related shortcuts.
- Unrealistic deadlines- Related to poor preplanning, unrealistic deadlines put unnecessary pressure on workers to perform. When deadlines force workers to rush, incidents and injuries are bound to occur overtime.
- Weather- Weather can throw a huge curve ball at production schedules in the construction industry. When weather is not planned for both in the short and long-term major issues and setbacks can arise for everyone involved.

Best Practices to Avoid Time-related Issues

Proper preplanning is critical to all work. New work tasks especially should be evaluated well ahead of the actual work needing to be completed. Tasks need to be evaluated for both safety issues and production issues. The hazards of the work need to be reviewed as well as what the mitigation actions would be for those hazards. Any extra safety equipment or training would need to be provided prior to the work beginning.

From a production standpoint, proper preplanning looks at what tools, material, equipment, personnel, time, etc. are needed to complete the project. Having all of these items in line prior to work beginning allows for a much smoother work process.

After preplanning is completed everyone should be on the same page of what time is required to complete the project. Realistic goals should be set by management and understood by everyone involved in the work. Plans for setbacks, weather conditions, or other issues should be considered when planning for time needed.

Topic:		
Instructor:	Location:	
Printed Name	**Signature**	**Date**

Topic: Ladder Safety Talk

Ladders are an essential tool on many jobsites and at home across the United States. Because of their wide spread use and the inherent danger of working at heights, they are responsible for a large number of injuries both on and off the job. The U.S. Consumer Product Safety Commission reports there are an average of 165,000 injuries at home every year and the CDC reported there was over 50,000 injuries on the job resulting from ladders in 2011.

Ladder Injury Facts and Statistics

- In 2011, 113 workers died while using a ladder.
- 43% of fatal falls on the job from 2001 to 2011 involved a ladder.
- According to the BLS 50% of all ladder-related injuries occurred when the individual was climbing with objects in their hands.
- Fractures are the most common type of ladder-related injury.

Common Causes of Ladder Falls

1. Unsafe actions when using ladders– People often do not follow the safe work practices when using ladders. Standing on the top step of a ladder is a common and deadly practice. Other actions like climbing up a ladder carrying objects, leaning to reach for something, and attempting to move the ladder while still on it are some common practices that lead to injuries.

2. No inspection prior to use– Problems such as cracked or broken rungs, loose bolts, non-approved fixes, etc. lead to injuries.

3. Not using the correct ladder– People will often use the same ladder for many different jobs and situations. Choosing a ladder that is too short for the job is often a problem that leads to an injury. Also choosing a ladder not stable enough for the ground conditions or one that is not rated properly for the job are issues that can lead to injury.

Ladder Safe Work Practices

- Never stand on the top step if it is not designed to be a step.
- Do not lean or reach to grab something while on a ladder. Climb down and reposition the ladder closer to the object or area you were trying to reach.
- Do not carry objects up the ladder in your hands. Use a tool belt or a retrieval system to bring tools up to you once you have climbed the ladder. Always have your hands free when climbing so you are able to have three points of contact with the ladder.
- Always inspect a ladder before use. If there is any problems with it, immediately tag it out of use and find a properly functioning ladder.
- Use the correct ladder for the job. There are many types of ladders to work in different situations. Check weight ratings to ensure you do not overload the ladder during use.
- Always secure the ladder. Make sure the ladder is stable on the ground before climbing up. Tie off the ladder to the structure you are next to. Have someone hold the ladder to secure it.

Topic:		
Instructor:	Location:	
Printed Name	**Signature**	**Date**

Topic: Pinch Points and Hand Injuries Safety Talk

We use our hands for virtually all work tasks that we do. Because of how often we use our hands, they are put in the line of fire where they can be injured. Hand injuries are the second leading type of injury on the job in the United States. A major type of injury to the hands and fingers on the job result from crushed-by type incidents. Pinch points are a hazard that lead to crushed-by injuries.

Pinch Points

A pinch point is defined as any point where it is possible for a body part to be caught between moving and stationary portions of equipment. Pinch points are found in many places throughout a workplace. Tasks such as equipment maintenance, lifting materials, assembly line work, and hooking up trailers are just a few common tasks where pinch points are a common hazard.

Safeguards to Avoid Pinch Points

- Eliminate the hazard by ensuring proper guarding is in place.
- Pay attention to where your hands are around any moving parts or any objects that have the potential to move.
- Do not place your hands where you cannot see them.
- Wear the proper gloves for whatever work task you are completing to reduce the amount of damage to your hands if they do end up in the line of fire.
- When working on equipment or machinery ensure they are properly locked out and tagged out to prevent unexpected start up.
- Properly block any equipment or parts where stored energy could be released.
- When working with others make sure to communicate to let each other know if you are out of the line of fire before moving objects or starting up equipment.

Summary

Often times it is not the obvious pinch points that injure a person such as a conveyor belt or a piece of moving machinery. Many times tasks as simple as shutting a truck door will end up in a pinch point injury due to a person not paying attention to where their hands are. It is important to not get complacent and monitor where your hands are when you complete any task.

Topic:

Instructor: | Location:

Printed Name	Signature	Date

Topic: Workplace Inspections Safety Talk

Workplace inspections are a basic necessity of any safety program. These inspections should be done prior to the start of work as well as periodically throughout the shift and at the end of the work task. Workplace inspections serve the purpose of identifying any hazards in a work area. After hazards are identified, they need to be corrected before work proceeds or continues. There can always additional hazards present in any work area that were not planned for.

Hazards in the Work Area

Objects, equipment, people, or even animals find their way into work areas disrupting the work and creating additional hazards. Elimination of hazards is the most effective way to avoid injuries and property damage incidents. It is important to remove any unnecessary people, items, or equipment prior to the start of a work task.

By removing unnecessary personnel from a work area there are less people that have the chance to interfere with the work or be in the line of fire if something were to go wrong. Objects that are not needed in the area create trip hazards or can be struck by moving equipment and should be moved as well. Biological hazards such as insects or wildlife in work areas can pose many hazards to workers. Insects such as ticks or spiders can carry disease or poison that can affect an individual for years. Insects and wildlife can also distract employees from their work which could cause an injury.

Inspection Focuses

There are many other hazards that can affect a work area. Some of the common items you should look for during a work place inspection include: fire hazards, faulty equipment, broken tools, housekeeping issues, missing equipment guards, electrical cord and outlet problems, sharp objects, and missing labels. These are just a few examples- think of hazards unique to your work tasks.

Summary

There can be a variety of issues in any single work area. It is important to take the time to thoroughly check your work area for hazards and take the steps to mitigate them. Eliminate as many hazards as you can before relying on a less efficient control to protect yourself such as PPE.

Topic:		
Instructor:	Location:	
Printed Name	**Signature**	**Date**

Topic: Grinders

Grinders use powered rotating attachments to work metal and other materials. Bench grinders are mounted to a bench or tabletop while pedestal grinders are mounted to the floor on a pedestal. With an abrasive, wire brush, or buffing wheel attachment, grinders sharpen tools and shape, clean, or polish metal pieces. Grinders can cause severe injuries to hands, fingers, eyes and face if they are not used correctly.

Don't wear gloves that could get pulled into rotating grinder parts along with your fingers and hand. Remove jewelry from around your neck, fingers, and wrists. Wear close-fitting clothing that will not get entangled in the moving parts. Tie back or secure long hair under a cap so your hair doesn't get entangled and pull your face into the grinder. Wear safety goggles and/or a face shield to prevent flying debris from cutting your face or getting lodged in your eye.

Check your grinder for safety before each use. It should be securely and permanently mounted to the bench or floor for stability. Don't "C" clamp portable grinders to a bench. They need to be securely fastened to prevent vibration. The electric supply to the grinder should be properly grounded to prevent shocks. The grinder should have an individual on/off switch for the safest controls. If the grinder is not in good working order, do not use it.

Follow the manufacturer's directions on proper wheel installation. Inspect the wheel and "ring" or "tap" test it to ensure that it is sound before you install it. Tighten nuts securely so the wheels don't fall off while you are working. Allow a newly installed wheel to run before you use it to grind to ensure that it is sound. Use the correct wheel attachments for your grinder. Wheels should have an RPM rating that matches the RPM rating of the grinder motor. Use the correct type of wheel for the material you are grinding. Store wheels so that they are not subject to the environment or damage.

Guarding is extremely important for safe grinder operation. Side guards should cover the spindle, nut, flange and wheel. Use a work rest that is adjusted to within 1/8-inch of the wheel. Adjust the tongue guard to within ¼ inch of the topside of the wheel. When the grinder is off and completely stopped, adjust the work rest and tongue guard to maintain these distances. When you can no longer adjust the work rest or tongue guard to maintain proper clearance, replace the wheel.

Don't start the grinder with your materials against the wheel; wait for the grinder to speed up and then apply the material. Place your material or item on the front face of the wheel, not the side. Keep your hands and fingers at least two inches away from the grinding surface. To avoid the risk of electric shock, dip tools and material into water to cool, don't apply water to the wheel.

Periodically sweep around grinders to maintain good housekeeping. Ground metal pieces can be very slippery, so consider a slip-resistant floor mat or flooring surface coating around the grinding bench. For grinders that produce large amounts of dust, consider a dust collector, exhaust hood, and/or respiratory protection. For fire safety, don't grind aluminum; use a belt sander. Avoid grinding magnesium because the dust can be extremely flammable.

Topic:		
Instructor:	Location:	

Printed Name	Signature	Date

Topic: Power Press

A power press can present serious hazards to its operator. A power press injury can result in the amputation of fingers, hands, or arms and cause other disabling injuries. Proper safeguards, employee training, press maintenance, and inspections are vital to the prevention of injuries.

A power press can be used in more than one production system and there may be several ways to safeguard each system. For operators, the greatest danger is at the point where stock is inserted, held, or withdrawn by hand. Safeguards are designed to eliminate the possibility of the operator or other workers from placing hands or any other body part from making contact with hazardous moving parts. Operators should never remove or tamper with safeguards.

A power press can be made safe but only its user can prevent machine guarding injuries. Press operators must receive a minimum of eight hours of on-the-job training under supervision before being assigned to operate a press. Operators of complex equipment may need two weeks or more of training before they run the equipment alone. Those working with presence-sensing device initiation equipment must receive training at least annually.

Press operators must know how to use press controls, where possible pinch points or moving parts are located, and where safety devices are located. Operators should be trained to lock out machinery, lubricate it, remove stuck work, and know to whom they should report any problems. Training should also include why, when, and how too use personal protective equipment.

Supervisors must understand all the hazards associated with power presses, how the safeguards work, and how to adjust them. They must check the setup and ensure that each operator has been properly trained. Supervisors should visually inspect each press at the start of a shift or whenever a new operator comes on duty. Each press must be inspected weekly to be sure that all functions are operating properly; and periodically, an in-depth inspection must be conducted.

Topic:		
Instructor:	Location:	
Printed Name	**Signature**	**Date**

Topic: Machine Guarding

Introduction

Machine guarding is a very important safety control. Guarding can protect against:

Debris, particulates and other projectiles from flying out of the machine

Pinch-points caused by moving components

People from entering energized work areas

Machines or components within machines from inadvertently shifting or moving during operations

Sparks, electrical arcs and internal fires from expanding beyond a controlled area within the machine

Whipping from broken belts and other materials under high tension or stress

Using ventilation systems and hoods to reduce or prevent inhalation of hazardous fumes

Using retaining walls, enclosures and spill containment devices to prevent chemicals, objects and other materials from reaching undesirable areas

Guidelines for ensuring machine guarding are effective:

Ensure the guarding is properly fastened or anchored and not loose.

Verify the guarding is strong enough to withstand the expected forces.

If the guarding is perforated (for example a fence) then the holes in the guarding should be smaller than the smallest object that could fly from the machine.

Always inspect and verify the guarding is adequate before operating the machine.

Topic:		
Instructor:	Location:	
Printed Name	**Signature**	**Date**

Topic: Machine Guards

Machine guards are designed to protect you when working with dangerous equipment. Unfortunately, many workers also view them as an inconvenience or an obstacle to the task at hand.

Protecting Against Hazards

Specifically, machine guards are used to protect against:

- Direct contact with moving parts
- Flying chips or other debris
- Kickbacks
- Splashing of metal or harmful liquids
- Mechanical and electrical failures
- Any number of potential human errors

While guards may often appear to be a hindrance, overall they have proven to be otherwise for both security and production. Greater machine speeds are made possible through proper guarding, as production does not have to stop due to injuries and employees can often work quicker knowing they have the proper protection in place to do so safely.

Types of Guards

Two types of guards are used to protect machine operators: fixed guards and interlocking guards. Fixed guards are most commonly used and are generally preferred because they protect you from dangerous parts of machines at all times. Interlocking guards are used if a fixed guard is not practical. This type will not allow the machine to operate until dangerous parts are guarded. The interlocking guard is designed to disconnect the source of power from the machine.

Safety devices such as pullbacks, sweeps and electronic devices are used where neither a fixed nor an interlocking guard can be used satisfactorily. Safety devices are operated by the machine itself. Regardless of the type of guard or safety device used, all provide the operator with the greatest possible protection.

Safety is Not an Option

Of course, no guard can do the job without the cooperation of the machine operator. Machine guards are a part of our workplace, and using them properly is your responsibility. Always follow these basic safety requirements:

- Do not adjust or remove a guard unless permission is given by your supervisor or unless the adjustment is a normal and accepted part of your job.
- Do not start machinery without the guards in place.
- If guards are missing or defective, report it to your supervisor immediately.
- If guards are removed for repair or adjustment, the power for the machine should be turned off and the main switch locked and tagged.
- Loose clothing, watches, rings and other jewelry should not be worn around mechanical equipment, and long hair should be tied back.

Safety is a top priority.

To accomplish this, we need the commitment of all employees to respect our safety rules and to use machine guards as intended, to keep everyone on the job safe and productive. If you have any questions regarding guards or other safety issues, please ask your supervisor.

Topic:		
Instructor:	Location:	
Printed Name	**Signature**	**Date**